*For my grandchildren who, in time,
will choose that very special someone —
to love and to cherish.*

To Love and To Cherish

MEDITATIONS FOR THE BRIDE

Dorene Waggoner

illustrated by Betsy Beach

The C. R. Gibson Company, Norwalk, Connecticut 06856

Excerpt from "On Marriage" reprinted from THE
PROPHET, by Kahlil Gibran, by permission of
Alfred A. Knopf, Inc. Copyright 1923 by Kahlil
Gibran and renewed 1951 by Administrators C.T.A.
of Kahlil Gibran Estate and Mary G. Gibran.

Text copyright © MCMLXXXVI by Dorene Waggoner
Art copyright © MCMLXXXVI by C.R. Gibson
Published by the C.R. Gibson Company
Norwalk, Connecticut 06856
Printed in the United States of America
ISBN 0-8378-5094-0

To the bride…

You are about to embark on one of life's most exciting and challenging adventures—marriage. God has prepared you for the special privilege that is marriage. He has given you the ability to love, to nurture, and to share. He has sent you a special person to be your partner for life. Place your hand in God's as you walk forward into the wonderful world of marriage.

I wish you happiness beyond measure and peace that passes all understanding.

Dorene Waggoner

Who Am I?

I see a mirror image of a woman. I am privileged because God created me in His own image, bestowing upon me a living soul. He has given me the ability to acquire knowledge and, through His grace, wisdom. I can accomplish great and wondrous things in this life—that is my own special gift.

I live and move and have my being in God. He has filled me with talent, skill, imagination, and energy. The mysteries of life flow through my veins. I will live life to the fullest, possessing each God-given day.

God's greatest gift to me is the power to be—to be His best. Within me has awakened a new sense of adventure. Within me I hold the power to love, serve, and inspire, to be giving and forgiving, sensitive and kind, joyous and tolerant.

He has given me power to claim the promise of love and, in return, to give that promise to another. I am so excited and happy. I am also frightened. Lord, you give us such a tremendous task when you proclaim in Your Word: *The two shall be as one flesh.* (Genesis 2:24) Lord, teach us the full meaning of these words as we enter this new world of marriage.

Soon we shall belong together. Soon our lives will be entwined in a mixture of love, passion, and belonging as never before.

We are beginning a lifelong venture together with You, Lord. I pray You will keep my beloved and me gentle and understanding, ready and eager to please each other, with a dash of humor to ease difficult moments.

Deep in my inner self, I feel an exciting calmness, a steadfastness flowing smoothly and gently as I prepare to take my first step into the unknown world of marriage. Marriage is experienced by millions, yet for each couple the path is new and untraveled, each mountain and valley unique to only two. But I know if we walk our marriage path hand in hand with God, our mountain tops will be smoother and our valleys will be greener.

Who am I? I am God's child—becoming an adult. Growing into womanhood is my birthright. To travel the pathway of marriage is my very special privilege.

Jesus said:

*Have ye not read, that he which
made them at the beginning made them
male and female…
Wherefore they are no more twain, but
one flesh. What therefore God hath
joined together, let not man put
asunder.*

Matthew 19:4, 6

My heart is like a singing bird
Whose nest is in a watered shoot;
My heart is like an apple-tree
Whose boughs are bent with thickest fruit;
My heart is like a rainbow shell
That paddles in a halcyon sea;
My heart is gladder than all these
Because my love is come to me.

Because the birthday of my life
Is come, my love is come to me.

Christina Rossetti

This Thing Called Love

Love is patient and kind...
bears all things
believes all things
hopes all things
endures all things
Love never fails.

I Corinthians 13:4, 7-8

God's Greatest Gift

Love is the greatest gift God has given us, my beloved, for God Himself is love. It is therefore the greatest gift we can give to God and to others. In loving each other, we will give ourselves and all that is ours. Love is the invisible force that will fuse our two minds, two hearts, and two spirits into one, yet leave us two separate and distinct beings.

To love someone to the fullest is to desire to help that person to grow and reach her or his highest potential. This is what we will strive for, my love, for the ability to love and to be loved is the one supreme good in human life.

A Lasting Flame

Let our love be real love—not simply "love at first sight"—
the kind we read about in romantic novels, see in movies, or
hear about in love songs. We know that bright, dancing
flames can be seen from new wood, but they soon dwindle
to a flicker. It is the seasoned wood that gives continued
warmth through its steady flame and glowing embers.

My prayer is that our love, given time to grow and
mature, will be like the seasoned wood, warming us to our
depths and allowing us to share our deepest hopes, doubts,
and fears. It is in this sharing, this truth, that our love will
grow into a brilliant, lasting flame.

Love Never Fails

There is a love that never fails and results in the full growth of
both the loved and the loving. Paul describes this in Colossians
3:14: *...above all put on love which binds everything together
in perfect harmony.*

Let us put on a love that binds, my beloved, like the love
that God has for us. May ours be not merely a romantic love
but a spiritual love, too.

What True Love Means To Me

True love is to be prized and cherished. It has the ability to give us emotional wealth and possesses the gift of inner youth. It is sure to have its ups and downs. The world's greatest music possesses highs and lows, and some mono- tone, too.

True love is something that allows us at times to lead and at times to follow. Love thrives on the freedom of the two individuals within its circle; it provides a sanctuary, a refuge from the racing world, a place of simple truth, and a place to be ourselves, the best selves we can be.

True love is like a gentle breeze. We cannot see it, but its touch refreshes us. True love is finding time to love, to share, to embrace the present and step boldly forward, together, into the future.

True love is gazing at your sleeping loved one, realizing that person is part of you, to understand, nurture, and sus- tain. It is sitting together in the quiet darkness, remembering things past, anticipating a smiling future.

True love is lending a listening ear to help cast away anxieties that chip away at happiness and joy; including in your union the true Creator of your love—God.

How do I love thee? Let me count the ways.
I love thee to the depth and breadth and height
My soul can reach, when feeling out of sight
For the ends of Being and ideal Grace.
I love thee to the level of every day's
Most quiet need, by sun and candlelight.
I love thee freely, as men strive for Right;
I love thee purely, as they turn from Praise.
I love thee with the passion put to use
In my old griefs, and with my childhood faith.
I love thee with a love I seemed to lose
With my lost saints, I love thee with the breadth,
Smiles, tears of all my life!—and, if God choose,
I shall but love thee better after death.

Elizabeth Barrett Browning

Marriage—
The Link That Binds

To Me Marriage Is—

So much more than a wedding ceremony, a bridal bouquet, a wedding cake, and a honeymoon. It is so much more than staying married.

A solemn covenant between two people and God. It carries with it endless possibilities for emotional growth and spiritual achievement.

The planting of new seeds of mutual love and respect.

Gaining a new companion, a new friend, a confidant, a partner. It is a commitment that can be fun, funny, solemn, romantic, breathless, and rewarding. In all respects, it is a challenge, and its success is the height of achievement.

Seeing the best in the other person. It gives the benefit of doubt and allows a steady love to flourish, even when imperfections are there.

An adventure that when approached with an adventurous attitude adds to life a glowing light of newness.

Two persons developing a mature acceptance of each other, each respecting the worth and dignity of the other, and realizing that thoughts and values may be shared, but never forced upon the other.

A oneness in mind, in heart, and in spirit. Oneness in mind is necessary, oneness in love is essential, but to live life fully, as God intended, oneness in spirit is also fundamental.

Not simply living for and with each other—it is two persons uniting and joining hands to serve God.

Marriage is—

> Sharing and caring,
> loving and being loved,
> walking hand in hand,
> giving and forgiving,
> talking heart to heart,
> seeing through each other's eyes,
> laughing together,
> weeping together,
> always trusting and believing,
> always being thankful to God for each other.

Let Us Celebrate Life!

Opening New Doors

My love and I hold jointly the key to a successful marriage. At times we will open our own individual doors; at other times we will open doors together. Behind these doors we may find joy, tears, or surprises. But we pray that the love that binds us will be a tough love, a maturing love that stands firm in times of triumph and in times of tragedy.

It is when love is deeply rooted that we find we can freely celebrate life to the fullest. My life is such a very brief span in the world's existence. God tells us this in Psalms (see Psalm 90:5-12) when he reminds us our life is,

> *Like grass which groweth up.*
> *In the morning it flourisheth,*
> *and groweth up;*
> *in the evening it is cut down,*
> *and withereth.*

So let us celebrate life! Let us use our days on earth in a way that makes our existence special. Each day is God's gift to us, a challenge, a new beginning. Let us leave the haunts of yesterday and the worries of tomorrow in God's care and live today to the fullest.

Let us celebrate life with *respect*—
> by realizing we are two separate and different people, possessing different lives, ideas, backgrounds. We belong *with* each other, but not *to* each other.

Let us celebrate life with *trust*—
> believing in our love even in darkest times. Let us search for understanding of whatever troubles us and, with trust and courage, work together to find solutions.

Let us celebrate life with *confidence*—
> by freeing each other to new and different worlds. Let the marriage be steadfast enough to take root and yet free enough to soar.

Let us celebrate life with *giving*—
> without thought of return, because we are not impoverished by the love we give, but made richer.

Let us celebrate life with *understanding*—
    not only in words, but in unspoken ways. A tender
    touch, a smile, can often say so much more than words.

Let us celebrate life with *forgiveness*—
    overlooking our human flaws, not expecting perfection
    in each other or in ourselves. And let us gain wisdom
    from the mistakes we make.

Let us celebrate life with *sharing*—
    stepping into the world together, expanding our circle
    of love to include friends, family, and others. Let our
    love radiate outward, touching the lives of all we meet.

Let us celebrate life with *quietness*—
    setting aside time together for peaceful soul-searching,
    Bible study, prayer and meditation, letting the annoy-
    ances of the day slip away into the calming hands of Jesus.

My Love, My Friend

The most powerful and lasting love is one that includes friendship. Let us begin our marriage as friends, my love, my partner. Through this sharing may we be drawn closer to God.

What is a friend?

> A friend is someone with whom we feel comfortable; someone we can count on for help and honest answers.

> A friend stands by us when we are hurting, sharing our struggles and pain.

> A friend believes in us and shares our dreams.

> A friend rejoices in our successes and comforts us in our failures.

> A friend grows with us, yet gives us space to grow alone.

> A friend is fun.

> A friend lends support and courage when we begin a new venture.

> A friend takes us as we are—accepting both our strengths and weaknesses.

> A friend is a true gift from God.

> So be my friend, my love.

This is my beloved, and this is my friend.

Song of Solomon 5:16

Love's Journey

Come run with me;
  Walk with me
Through fields of
  New mown hay.
Let me feel
  My hand in yours;
Share the gladness
  Of the day.

Come sit by me
  In quietness;
Enfold me in
  A warm embrace.
Fill me with a
  Confident joy;
Touch my lips;
  Caress my face.

Speak to me
Of gentle things,
Of secret dreams,
Of hope and fear,
Of joy, of love,
and laughter,
Of deepest thoughts
The heart to cheer.

And in our sharing
And our knowing,
We'll find a tender
Love is growing.

Dorene Waggoner

Sharing Space

A Garden that Blooms

Our marriage will not only be a union of two individuals, it will be also a union of two separate spirits with the Spirit of God. It is our two whole persons coming together. I pray, Lord, that our union will bring out the best of our two earthly natures. Let our marriage be a garden that blooms joyfully in every season. We will water it with affection, feed it with tender intimacy, and strengthen it with mutual respect and unshakable confidence. In our marriage, we are committing ourselves to share our earthly space with each other. We will not be giving up our freedom; we will not stop growing. We will be adding different freedoms and allowing ourselves an even greater potential for growth.

God at the Center

I picture a wedding band. My love and I hold hands to form a circle. In the center of our circle is God. We are linked together, yet each of us stands alone in his or her own space, with God at the center of our union.

Our marriage, with God's help, will be one that allows each of us to learn, to grow, to respond, and to listen.

"I Understand"

But we must not expect our marriage to be endless bliss; it cannot, no more than can life. Life is made up of all seasons and so is marriage.

When space is shared by two persons, there will, from time to time, be conflict and clashing of ideas. Through love, we will work out these conflicts and, in doing so, we will grow and become stronger partners. Let us work things through until we are able to say, "I understand."

We will take time to look for solutions. Let us pray that our marriage will be strengthened not by being freed from difficulty, but by allowing God to help us work out the difficulties that are part of living together.

A Touch of Humor

The marriage ceremony will not change two people from imperfect to perfect. We will learn things about each other that will be surprising and sometimes annoying. Living together for twenty-four hours a day can be a most revealing experience!

We all have our idiosyncracies—little annoying habits that can get on our loved one's nerves. These things don't fade away. Ignoring them won't help, and tension can build. Let us talk about these things and be giving and forgiving. Let us work together to learn the art of patience. Let us pray together for acceptance and understanding of each other's flaws. Working through this is part of growing up and growing into marriage. Above all, let us learn to laugh together. Many a tense situation is defused by stepping back for a moment and seeing the humor in a situation.

Being Ourselves

Let us give freely of ourselves, for sharing is not really sharing when we give only our possessions. Let us joyfully share ourselves, opening our hearts fully to each other. May we be trusting—comfortable enough to drop all pretenses—sharing our thoughts and feelings and never indulging in game playing.

Love is the process of being joined together, hand in hand, yet remaining separate individuals. Yet it will not be necessary, or even good, for us to spend all our waking, non-working hours together. There will be times when each of us will need to be alone. This is not a lonely state, but a time to reflect, to dream, to pursue individual interests, to strengthen our inner selves. These times of separateness will serve to strengthen our bond and enhance our times of togetherness.

But let there be space in your
togetherness,
And let the winds of the
heavens dance between you.

Love one another, but make
not a bond of love;
Let it rather be a moving sea
between the shores of your soul.
Fill each other's cup but drink
not from one cup.
Give one another of your bread
but eat not from the same loaf.
Sing and dance together and be
joyous, but let each one of you be alone,
Even as the strings of a lute are alone
though they quiver with the same music.

Kahlil Gibran

Finding Rainbows

A Host of Treasures

When we open our hearts to another person, we discover the rainbows of life—a host of treasures that the Bible calls the fruit of the spirit. These are *love, joy, peace, patience, gentleness, goodness, faith, meekness, and self-control.* (See Galatians 5:22-23)

If we place these with St. Paul's love chapter (I Corinthians 13) we find the brilliant hues of the rainbow shining through.

Patience	—Love is patient
Kindness	—and kind
Gentleness	—love is not jealous or boastful
Goodness	—nor is it arrogant or rude
Self-Control	—love does not insist on its own way
Faithful	—love is not irritable or resentful
Peaceful	—does not rejoice in wrong
Joyful	—but rejoices in the right.

Let us reach for these God-given rainbows and use them when we need them. Each is equally important in itself, but when linked together the chain is indestructible.

Discovering Ourselves

How exciting to look at the one we love and realize that we will share with that person a lifetime of love, of joy, of tears, and of wonder.

Some people live long lives but never discover themselves. To be a truly loving person, we must first know and love ourselves. Let us always look inside to discover our own rainbows.

In our voyage of self-discovery we find many things within us—love, talents, tears, joy, fears, peace. Each of these dimensions is wonderful in its own way. Each must grow continually to enable us to achieve our full potential. Each of us has something special to share and the wonder of sharing is that the more we share, the more we have to share.

Joining Hands and Hearts

Let us not miss the beautiful rainbow of togetherness. Eating a banquet alone cannot compare with sharing a sandwich with the one you love. How much more wonderful to stroll through the park and experience nature in all her glory together! How much more powerful to join hands and hearts and souls in thanksgiving to God, the Creator of all good and perfect gifts.

Let us look for rainbows. If we look for the best, expect the best, we will find the best and, just as surely, we will give our best in return. Let us joyfully invest our time and energy in our marriage, because lasting marriages don't just happen, they are built, hour by hour, day by day.

Be thou the rainbow to the storms of life;
the evening beam that smiles the clouds away,
and tints tomorrow with prophetic ray.

George Gordon Byron

Loving—
In Word And In Deed

A Kind Word

I pray we will never substitute actions for words, or words for actions in our marriage. Both are equally important. Let us ask ourselves often, "What can I do to make my beloved happy?" By our words and actions let us speak to each other, reaching to the depths of each other's hearts.

How marvelous it would be to have a "courting" marriage! In times of courtship, we are always anxious to please. We want to dress right, to say and do all the right things at all the right times. Is it not so much more important to do these things when we are married—when we are as one?

To share this glorious togetherness, let us tread softly and fill our days with words of love, of strength, and of encouragement. Let us always be ready and willing to give a kind word and be ever slow to pass out words of criticism. When we feel like criticizing, I pray we may be able to stop and focus on each other's good points.

Created Out of Love

God created us out of love, to love, and to be loved. Life really begins when we are able to receive unlimited love from another and to dare to give it in return. Let us both remember to speak kindly of each other and find ways to show our love not only by words, but by actions, too.

One of the most damaging things to any love relationship is the "if" condition. "I will love you IF you make good grades, IF you change your job, IF you change your personality." I pray we will not put limits or conditions on our love, on our time, or on our concern.

Talking it Out

We should never be afraid of disagreements or arguments. It has been said that the only people who don't disagree either don't care or are dead. Let us make sure our disagreement is over, finished, and then let us forget it.

Let us keep our disagreements behind closed doors, but let us also remember that our home is not a place of strife. Our home is where we will both find comfort and acceptance, no matter how difficult the day. It is a place full of warm, caring love, a place to mend the heart, a place to ease the pain and to gain the strength to face another day. True happiness is found in the home where there is unconditional love. A cheerful outlook and a positive attitude are vital to a happy home. No matter how hard the day or how tired we feel, if we show love and respect for each other, our home will be a haven, a resting place where we can be renewed and replenished.

Gentle Love

Home is where a gentle love is shown in a touch, a word, a hug, a tear, a smile. This love can be full of excitement, joy, blessed silence, or intense emotion, but at its core, it is always a gentle love. Gentle love can be felt in the deepest storehouse of our hearts, in a touch, a glance, or a deep, longing search through the hills and valleys of the soul.

Growing Love

May we always remember that love is not static, but moving and growing. Human relationships change and if we are to grow in the relationship, we must be willing to change.

Let us learn to laugh at our mistakes. Laughter smooths the sharp edges of life. Laughing with each other but not at each other balances that "too serious" attitude that sometimes creeps over all of us. Laughter gives life a sparkle and helps keep perfectionism and unrealistic expectations at bay.

Today is the Day

Above all else, my love, let us promise never to put off till tomorrow what can be said and done today. Today is the day to *say*, "I love you." It is the day to *show* "I love you." Today is the day to touch each other, to laugh together, to cry together, to explore the world together. We do not know how many tomorrows we will have.

And as we reach the gentle, mellow season of life, I pray we will be able to look into each other's eyes and still find newness, still see our life together as a wonderful adventure, with new mountains to climb and new valleys to explore.

Designed by Betsy Beach
Type set in Galliard and Galliard Italic
Calligraphy by Wulf Stapelfeldt